MILLIONAIRE AT 20

THE MASTER PLAN TO EARLY FINANCIAL SUCCESS

OKAH ABRAHAM O

ISBN: **9798863241449**

DEDICATION

This book is dedicated to my family and friends including those who has not found my content.

CONTENTS

CHAPTER ONE

INTRODUCTION

1.0 The Power of Early Financial Success

In the grand scheme of life, wealth and financial success are aspirations many of us share. There's something undeniably alluring about the idea of having the resources to live life on our terms, free from the shackles of financial constraints. Yet, what sets this book apart is not just the pursuit of financial success, but the timing of it. It's about aiming for millionaire status while still in your twenties.

In this opening chapter, we embark on a journey that explores the transformative power of early financial success. We'll uncover the remarkable advantages it offers and the profound impact it can have on your life and the lives of those around you. Let's begin.

The Time Advantage

Time is a resource as valuable as money itself. Imagine it as the fertile soil in which your financial seeds are planted. The earlier you start, the longer your investments have to grow. This is the essence of compound interest, a phenomenon where your money earns money on itself.

To illustrate this point, consider two hypothetical investors: Alex and Ben. Alex begins investing at 20 and puts away $5,000 per year for ten years, for a total investment of $50,000. Ben, on the other hand, waits until he's 30 to start investing and puts away $5,000 per year for thirty years, also a total investment of $150,000. Assuming both earn an average annual return of 7%, who do you think ends up with more money at age 60?

The answer might surprise you. Alex, who invested for only ten years, ends up with approximately $602,070, while Ben, who invested for thirty years, accumulates around $540,741. Alex, despite investing less money and for a shorter period, comes out ahead, thanks to the magic of compound interest.

This example illustrates the time advantage you possess when you start building wealth early. The earlier you begin, the more time your investments have to compound and grow exponentially. It's like a snowball rolling downhill, gathering momentum and size as it goes.

Freedom and Flexibility

Imagine waking up each day with the freedom to choose how you spend your time. You're not bound by the necessity of earning a paycheck just to cover your bills. Instead, you have the liberty to pursue a career or venture you're passionate about, regardless of the income it initially provides.

Early financial success provides this freedom. It allows you to select a career or path based on your interests and values rather than being driven solely by financial necessity. Whether you aspire to be an artist, an environmentalist, a social entrepreneur, or any other passion driven professional, early financial success opens the door to these possibilities.

This isn't about avoiding work or responsibility. Instead, it's about working because you want to, not because you have to. It's about aligning your career with your calling, leading to a more fulfilling and purpose driven life.

Reduced Stress and Anxiety

Picture a life with reduced stress and anxiety about money. Bills and financial responsibilities no longer haunt your thoughts. You can focus on personal growth, relationships, and self-improvement without the constant burden of financial worry.

Financial stability at a young age brings peace of mind. It allows you to face life's challenges with confidence, knowing that you have a financial safety net. Unexpected expenses, such as medical bills or car repairs, become inconveniences rather than crises.

Moreover, reduced financial stress has a positive impact on your mental and physical health. Stress related health issues are less likely to plague your life, leading to a happier and healthier existence.

Opportunities for Generosity

Financial success brings with it the capacity to be

generous. Imagine having the resources to make a meaningful difference in your community or the world. Early financial success allows you to support causes you're passionate about, whether it's providing scholarships for underprivileged students, contributing to environmental conservation efforts, or helping eradicate poverty.

Giving back is not just about financial donations; it's about making a positive impact on the world. When you're financially secure, you can devote your time, energy, and resources to causes that matter most to you. This is where the true power of wealth becomes evident, not just in personal gain but in the ability to create a better world for others.

Setting a Strong Foundation

Early financial success lays the groundwork for future financial prosperity. It initiates a cycle of continued success and wealth accumulation. While the initial pursuit may be for personal gain, it often leads to benefits that extend to your family and future generations.

This concept is known as generational wealth. It's not just

about amassing riches for yourself but also about providing opportunities and financial security for your descendants. By setting a strong financial foundation, you create a legacy that can endure for generations to come.

Consider the impact of your financial decisions on your children and grandchildren. Your choices today can provide them with educational opportunities, a secure future, and the ability to pursue their own dreams without the burden of financial stress.

Inspiring Others

Finally, early financial success can serve as a source of inspiration for others. Your journey can become a beacon of hope and a testament to the possibilities that exist with determination, discipline, and smart financial choices.

When you achieve millionaire status in your twenties, you break the mold of conventional financial timelines. You show others that it's not necessary to follow the traditional path of working for decades before achieving financial security. Your success becomes a story of what's possible when you think differently about money and take deliberate steps to achieve your financial goals.

As we continue our exploration of early financial success in the following chapters, keep in mind the transformative power it holds. The advantages of time, freedom, reduced stress, opportunities for generosity, and the ability to set a strong foundation are all within your reach. This book is your guide, providing the knowledge, strategies, and inspiration to help you on your journey to becoming a millionaire at 20.

1.1 The Myth of the Overnight Millionaire

In this chapter, we'll debunk the myth of the overnight millionaire and delve into the realities of building wealth through sustainable and principled means. While it may seem like some individuals achieve millionaire status in the blink of an eye, these stories often overshadow the hard work, dedication, and time invested behind the scenes.

The Illusion of Instant Success

We live in an era where media, especially social media,

tends to glorify and sensationalize stories of instant success. We've all heard tales of individuals who seemingly became millionaires overnight—perhaps through winning the lottery, hitting a viral jackpot, or launching the next big app.

These stories, however, are the exception rather than the rule. They represent a small fraction of wealth accumulation cases. Relying on such tales as a master plan for your own financial journey is akin to buying a lottery ticket as your retirement plan—highly improbable and risky.

The Importance of Hard Work and Persistence

True financial success, especially at a young age, generally requires a substantial amount of hard work, dedication, and persistence. It's a journey marked by consistent effort, a willingness to learn from failures, and the ability to adapt to changing circumstances.

Consider the success stories of some of the world's most renowned entrepreneurs and business leaders. Behind their achievements are countless hours of labor, numerous setbacks, and relentless determination. Achieving millionaire status, particularly early in life, is seldom a result of chance; it's a reward for relentless pursuit.

2.3 Building Skills and Expertise

The overnight millionaire stories often overlook the years of preparation and skill development that led to the breakthrough moment. These individuals typically possess valuable skills and expertise in their respective fields, honed over time through education, training, and practical experience.

Whether you aim to succeed in business, investing, or any other pursuit, investing in your knowledge and skills is paramount. Skills and expertise are the foundation upon which you can build sustainable wealth. Remember, those who seem to achieve success overnight often spent years preparing for that moment.

Risk and Reward

Quick riches often come with significant risks. Stories of overnight success rarely convey the associated risks and potential downsides. For every instant millionaire, there are countless others who experienced financial ruin due to hasty decisions or ill-conceived ventures.

Understanding risk and reward is crucial to making informed financial decisions. Rather than relying on luck or speculation, successful wealth accumulation involves careful consideration of the risks involved and strategies to mitigate them.

The Role of Education and Knowledge

Education and continuous learning are vital components of financial success. Many overnight success stories feature individuals who possess deep knowledge and expertise in their chosen domains. This knowledge not only helps them seize opportunities but also navigate challenges effectively.

Investing in your financial education, whether through formal schooling or self-directed learning, is a fundamental step in your journey toward early financial success. Understanding personal finance, investing principles, and entrepreneurship can significantly impact your ability to make informed financial decisions.

Planning and Strategy

Behind most successful individuals who achieve wealth early in life is a well thought-out plan and strategy. Whether it's a business plan, an investment strategy, or a roadmap for achieving financial goals, planning plays a pivotal role.

In the subsequent chapters of this book, we'll explore the importance of financial planning and provide insights into creating your own roadmap to early financial success. A well-structured plan can guide your actions, helping you make strategic decisions and stay on course.

Avoiding Get Rich Quick Schemes

A common pitfall on the path to financial success is the allure of get rich quick schemes and scams. These schemes promise instant wealth but often lead to financial ruin.

They prey on the desire for easy riches and exploit the unsuspecting.

Throughout this book, we'll emphasize the importance of due diligence and responsible financial decision-making. Beware of anything that promises instant wealth without effort or risk, and instead, focus on building wealth through legitimate means.

Building Sustainable Wealth

Ultimately, true financial success isn't just about accumulating money; it's about preserving and growing it sustainably. Overnight millionaires who fail to manage their newfound wealth effectively often find themselves back where they started, or worse.

Wealth building involves prudent financial management, including budgeting, saving, investing, and risk management. It's about creating a solid financial foundation that can withstand economic fluctuations and provide longterm security.

Realistic Expectations

By the end of this chapter, it's crucial to have a realistic perspective on the journey to early financial success. While quick success stories may grab headlines, they don't represent the norm. The path to millionaire status early in life is typically characterized by hard work, smart financial decisions, and perseverance.

Set achievable goals and understand that financial success is a result of deliberate effort. It's not a matter of instant gratification but rather a journey that rewards discipline and persistence.

Conclusion

In conclusion, "The Myth of the Overnight Millionaire" chapter serves as a reality check. It reminds you that while instant success stories exist, they are outliers. The path to early financial success is typically one of gradual progress, learning, and careful planning.

As you continue reading, remember that the true master plan for building wealth at a young age is based on principles, not luck. The subsequent chapters will provide you with practical strategies and principles that, when applied diligently, can lead you toward your goal of becoming a millionaire in your twenties.

1.3 Setting Realistic Goals

In this chapter, we delve into the fundamental process of setting clear and achievable financial goals. Your financial journey begins with a destination in mind, and setting realistic goals provides you with a roadmap for reaching your desired financial status.

The Significance of Goal Setting

Imagine embarking on a journey without a destination in mind. You'd wander aimlessly, with no sense of purpose or direction. Similarly, achieving financial success, especially at a young age, requires a clear destination—a set of goals that define your vision for the future.

Goals serve as the compass guiding your financial decisions and actions. They provide focus, motivation, and a sense of accomplishment as you work towards them.

Without goals, you're adrift in a sea of financial possibilities, making it challenging to make meaningful progress.

Short-term vs. Long-term Goals

Financial goals can be broadly categorized into short-term and long-term goals. Short-term goals typically have a horizon of one to three years and often involve immediate financial needs or desires. Long-term goals span over several years, sometimes decades, and encompass significant life objectives, such as retirement planning and wealth accumulation.

Short-term goals might include paying off credit card debt, saving for a vacation, or establishing an emergency fund. Long-term goals may involve buying a home, funding your children's education, or achieving financial independence and early retirement.

Balancing both short-term and long-term goals is essential. Short-term goals provide a sense of achievement and immediate financial security, while long-term goals ensure your financial future remains on track.

SMART Goals

Effective goal setting involves crafting SMART goals—Specific, Measurable, Achievable, Relevant, and Time bound. Let's break down these components:

Specific: Clearly define what you want to achieve. Vague goals like "get rich" lack specificity. Instead, specify the amount you want to save or invest and the timeline for achieving it.

Measurable: Your goals should be quantifiable. You should be able to track your progress and know when you've successfully achieved the goal. For instance, "save $10,000 by the end of next year" is measurable.

Achievable: Goals should be realistic and attainable based on your current financial situation and resources. Setting unrealistic goals can lead to frustration and disappointment.

Relevant: Ensure your goals align with your overall financial objectives and values. Ask yourself if the goal is meaningful and relevant to your life.

Time bound: Set a specific timeframe for achieving your goal. This adds urgency and helps you stay focused. "Pay off $5,000 in credit card debt within 12 months" is time bound.

Crafting SMART goals ensures that your goals are clear, actionable, and manageable, increasing your chances of success.

Prioritizing Goals

With limited resources—such as income, time, and energy—it's essential to prioritize your financial goals. Not all goals can be pursued simultaneously, so you must determine which ones are most critical and deserving of your attention.

A common framework for prioritizing goals is the "Needs, Wants, and Wishes" approach. Needs are essential, nonnegotiable expenses, such as housing, utilities, and groceries. Wants include discretionary spending on items like dining out or entertainment. Wishes are aspirational goals, like early retirement or starting a business.

By categorizing your goals into these three buckets, you can allocate your resources accordingly. Needs take precedence, followed by wants, and finally wishes. This approach ensures that you address immediate financial obligations while working toward long-term aspirations.

Goal Setting Exercises

To assist you in defining your financial goals, this chapter provides practical exercises and tools. These exercises encourage self-reflection and help you clarify your financial aspirations. Some of the exercises you'll find include:

Goal Mapping: Creating a visual representation of your financial goals and their interconnectedness.

Values Alignment: Assessing how your goals align with your personal values and priorities.

Timeframe Analysis: Evaluating the timeline for achieving specific goals and the impact of various deadlines.

These exercises empower you to tailor your goals to your unique circumstances, ensuring they resonate with your values and motivations.

Monitoring Progress

Setting goals is only the first step. To achieve them, you must regularly monitor your progress. Tracking your financial milestones allows you to stay on course and make necessary adjustments along the way.

Establish a system for monitoring your goals, whether through financial software, spreadsheets, or dedicated goal tracking apps. Regularly reviewing your progress reinforces your commitment and provides an opportunity to celebrate achievements.

Adjusting for Life Changes

Life is unpredictable, and circumstances change. Your goals and financial plans may need adjustment in response to life events such as career changes, family additions, or unexpected financial challenges.

Adaptability is a key trait of successful goal setters. Be prepared to modify your goals as needed, keeping your overarching financial objectives in mind. Flexibility ensures that your financial plan remains relevant and effective.

Celebrating Achievements

Recognizing and celebrating your financial milestones is an essential part of goal achievement. Celebrations provide motivation and a sense of accomplishment. Whether it's paying off a student loan, reaching a savings target, or achieving a specific investment milestone, take the time to acknowledge your progress.

Celebrate not only the destination but also the journey. Reflect on the hard work and discipline that went into achieving your goals. Celebrations serve as reminders of your ability to make meaningful financial progress.

Balancing Ambition and Realism

While setting ambitious goals is encouraged, it's also essential to maintain a balance between ambition and realism. Goals should challenge you but remain achievable with effort and dedication.

Balancing ambition and realism prevents you from becoming discouraged by overly ambitious goals that may seem insurmountable. It allows you to maintain a healthy sense of motivation and confidence in your ability to succeed.

Aligning Goals with Values

Lastly, it's crucial to consider how your financial goals align with your personal values. Aligning your goals with your core values provides a sense of purpose and motivation in your journey to early financial success.

When your financial objectives resonate with your values, they become more than mere numbers—they become expressions of what truly matters to you. This alignment can provide the motivation needed to stay committed to your goals, especially during challenging times.

Conclusion

The "Setting Realistic Goals" chapter emphasizes that goal setting is the cornerstone of financial success. Clear and achievable goals provide direction, motivation, and a sense of purpose in your financial journey.

As you continue reading, consider the exercises and principles discussed in this chapter to define your own financial goals. Remember that your goals should be SMART—Specific, Measurable, Achievable, Relevant, and Time bound. By setting realistic goals and aligning them with your values, you establish a solid foundation for your journey to becoming a millionaire at 20.

CHAPTER TWO

2.0 Financial Literacy

In this chapter, we delve into the critical topic of financial literacy—the foundation upon which sound financial decision-making is built. Financial literacy is not only a crucial skill but also a fundamental tool for achieving early financial success. In this chapter, we'll explore what financial literacy entails and provide practical guidance on how to enhance your financial knowledge.

2.1 Defining Financial Literacy

Financial literacy refers to the ability to understand and manage your personal finances effectively. It involves acquiring the knowledge, skills, and attitudes necessary to make informed and responsible financial decisions.

Key components of financial literacy include:

Budgeting: Creating and managing a budget to track income and expenses.

Savings: Developing strategies to save and invest money wisely.

Investing: Understanding investment options, risk management, and strategies to grow wealth.

Debt Management: Managing and reducing debt, including credit cards, loans, and mortgages.

Financial Planning: Creating a comprehensive financial plan to achieve your financial objectives.

Retirement Planning: Preparing for a secure and

comfortable retirement.

Risk Management: Understanding insurance, estate planning, and risk mitigation.

2.2 The Importance of Financial Literacy

Financial literacy is essential for several compelling reasons:

Empowerment

Financial literacy empowers individuals to take control of their financial futures. It equips you with the knowledge and confidence to make informed decisions about your money, from saving for emergencies to investing for retirement.

Wealth Accumulation

A solid foundation in financial literacy is a powerful tool for wealth accumulation. It enables you to make wise financial choices, such as investing intelligently, minimizing unnecessary expenses, and optimizing tax strategies.

Financial Security

Financial literacy is a critical component of achieving financial security. Understanding how to build emergency funds, manage insurance, and plan for unexpected expenses enhances your ability to navigate financial challenges with confidence.

Debt Management

Effectively managing debt is a vital aspect of financial literacy. It equips you with the skills to avoid excessive debt, pay down existing debts, and use credit responsibly.

Resilience

Financial literacy enhances your financial resilience. It prepares you to adapt to changes, recover from setbacks, and maintain financial stability even in challenging circumstances.

2.3 Building Financial Literacy

Building financial literacy is a continuous and empowering journey. Here are practical steps to enhance your financial knowledge:

2.3.1 Education

Read Books: Explore books on personal finance, investing, and wealth building.

Online Courses: Enroll in online courses or webinars offered by reputable institutions.

Seminars and Workshops: Attend financial seminars and workshops to learn from experts.

Certifications: Consider pursuing financial certifications like the Certified Financial Planner (CFP) or Chartered Financial Analyst (CFA).

2.3.2 Self-study

Online Resources: Utilize online resources such as financial websites, blogs, and forums.

Podcasts: Listen to podcasts on personal finance and investment topics.

Financial News: Stay informed about financial news and trends to understand their impact on your finances.

2.3.3 Financial Tools

Budgeting Apps: Use budgeting apps and tools to track income and expenses.

Investment Platforms: Familiarize yourself with investment platforms and tools for research and analysis.

Retirement Calculators: Use retirement calculators to plan for your future financial needs.

2.3.4 Seek Guidance

Financial Advisors: Consult with financial advisors or planners for personalized guidance.

Mentorship: Seek mentorship from individuals with expertise in finance and investing.

2.3.5 Practice

Real Life Practice: Apply what you've learned by making real financial decisions, such as creating a budget, investing in stocks, or managing debt.

2.4 Teaching Financial Literacy

Sharing your financial knowledge with others is a valuable way to reinforce your understanding and contribute to the financial literacy of your community. Consider:

Teaching: Offer financial literacy workshops or seminars in your community or workplace.

Mentoring: Mentor individuals, especially young adults, to help them develop financial literacy skills.

Family Education: Educate your family members, including children, about financial principles and responsible money management.

2.5 Conclusion

Financial literacy is not a destination; it's a lifelong journey. It's a commitment to understanding and managing your finances effectively. By continuously improving your financial knowledge and skills, you empower yourself to make sound financial decisions and work towards early financial success.

In the upcoming chapters, we will explore additional strategies and principles that, when combined with financial literacy, can accelerate your journey toward becoming a millionaire at 20.

CHAPTER THREE

3.0 Entrepreneurship

In this chapter, we explore the dynamic world of entrepreneurship and its pivotal role in achieving early financial success. Entrepreneurship isn't just about starting a business; it's a mindset and approach to creating value, identifying opportunities, and taking calculated risks. In this chapter, we'll delve into the entrepreneurial journey and how it can lead you toward your goal of becoming a millionaire at 20.

3.1 The Entrepreneurial Mindset

Entrepreneurship begins with a mindset—a way of thinking and approaching opportunities and challenges. Cultivating an entrepreneurial mindset is fundamental to your journey to financial success. Key attributes of the entrepreneurial mindset include:

Creativity: The ability to think outside the box and generate innovative ideas.

Risk Tolerance: A willingness to embrace calculated risks and face uncertainty.

Resilience: The capacity to bounce back from setbacks and learn from failures.

Adaptability: Being open to change and willing to adjust strategies as needed.

Vision: The ability to see opportunities where others may not and envision a better future.

Nurturing these qualities can empower you to identify and pursue entrepreneurial opportunities effectively.

3.2 Identifying Opportunities

Opportunities are the lifeblood of entrepreneurship. They can manifest in various forms, from unmet market needs to innovative product ideas or emerging trends. Identifying opportunities requires a keen eye, market research, and a deep understanding of your target audience.

To uncover opportunities, consider the following:

Market Research: Analyze industry trends, consumer behavior, and competition to identify gaps and unmet needs.

Problem Solving: Look for problems that people face daily and brainstorm solutions.

Passion and Expertise: Leverage your passions and areas of expertise to identify niches or opportunities you are uniquely positioned to explore.

Networking: Engage with mentors, industry experts, and peers who can provide insights and potentially introduce you to opportunities.

Remember that not all opportunities are created equal. Evaluate each one based on its potential for profitability, scalability, and alignment with your skills and interests.

3.3 Starting and Scaling a Business

Starting a business is a significant step toward early financial success. While entrepreneurship is rewarding, it's not without its challenges. Here's an overview of the key steps involved:

Step 1: Idea Validation

Validate your business idea by testing it with a small group of potential customers.

Gather feedback and refine your concept based on their input.

Step 2: Business Plan

Develop a comprehensive business plan outlining your business's structure, mission, market analysis, marketing strategy, financial projections, and more.

Step 3: Legal Structure and Registration

Choose a legal structure for your business, such as a sole proprietorship, partnership, LLC, or corporation.

Register your business with the appropriate authorities and obtain any necessary licenses or permits.

Step 4: Funding

Secure funding for your business through personal savings, loans, investors, or crowd funding.

Create a detailed financial plan to manage your startup costs and ongoing expenses.

Step 5: Branding and Marketing

Establish your brand identity, including your company name, logo, and messaging.

Develop a marketing strategy to reach and engage your target audience.

Step 6: Operations

Set up your business operations, including sourcing products or services, hiring staff, and establishing processes.

Step 7: Launch

Launch your business, promote your products or services, and start serving customers.

Step 8: Growth and Scaling

Continuously evaluate and refine your business strategy.

Explore opportunities for growth, such as expanding to new markets or diversifying your product offerings.

Entrepreneurship requires dedication, resilience, and a willingness to adapt to changing circumstances. It's a journey that involves both risks and rewards. Be prepared to learn from both your successes and failures.

3.4 The Power of Multiple Income Streams

Entrepreneurs often benefit from having multiple income streams. Diversifying your sources of income can provide financial stability and enhance your ability to achieve early financial success. These income streams may include:

Primary Business: Your core entrepreneurial venture.

Side Hustles: Additional income generating activities or businesses that complement your primary venture.

Investments: Income generated from investments, such as stocks, real estate, or bonds.

Passive Income: Earnings from assets or ventures that require minimal ongoing effort, such as royalties, dividends, or rental income.

Diversification reduces the risk associated with relying

solely on one income source. It can also accelerate your journey to millionaire status by increasing your overall earnings potential.

3.5 Risk Management

Entrepreneurship inherently involves risk. However, effective risk management is crucial for safeguarding your financial wellbeing. Here are key strategies to mitigate risk:

Market Research: Thoroughly research your target market and industry to identify potential risks and challenges.

Financial Planning: Create a robust financial plan that includes contingency funds to address unexpected expenses or downturns.

Insurance: Consider appropriate insurance coverage, such as liability insurance or business interruption insurance.

Legal Protection: Consult legal experts to ensure your business is compliant with regulations and protected from legal risks.

Diversification: As mentioned earlier, diversify your income streams to reduce reliance on a single source of revenue.

By actively managing risks, you can position yourself for sustainable success and early financial security.

3.6 Conclusion

Entrepreneurship is a powerful path toward achieving early financial success. It requires the right mindset, the ability to identify opportunities, and the courage to take calculated risks. While it comes with challenges, the rewards can be significant, offering not only financial prosperity but also the freedom and flexibility to live life on your terms.

As you continue your journey toward becoming a millionaire at 20, keep in mind that entrepreneurship is not a one size fits all approach. It's essential to tailor your entrepreneurial endeavors to your unique skills, passions, and goals. In the chapters ahead, we'll explore other avenues for wealth accumulation, allowing you to create a well-rounded strategy for achieving your financial aspirations.

CHAPTER FOUR

4.0 Investing

In this chapter, we dive into the world of investing, a fundamental component of wealth accumulation and financial success. Investing wisely is a key factor on the path to becoming a millionaire at a young age. We'll explore various aspects of investing, including strategies, asset classes, risk management, and the importance of a long term perspective.

4.1 The Power of Investing

Investing is the process of allocating your money with the expectation of generating a return or profit in the future. It's a powerful tool for growing wealth, and it plays a central role in achieving financial success. Here are key reasons why investing is crucial:

Wealth Accumulation: Investing allows your money to work for you, potentially earning a return on your capital and accelerating your path to financial independence.

Inflation Hedge: Investing can help your money keep pace with or outpace inflation, ensuring that your purchasing power remains strong over time.

Passive Income: Certain investments, like stocks that pay dividends or rental properties, can provide passive income streams, increasing your financial security.

Diversification: Through investing in different asset classes, you can diversify your portfolio, spreading risk and potentially enhancing returns.

4.2 Investment Strategies

Successful investing requires a well-defined strategy that aligns with your financial goals, risk tolerance, and time horizon. Some common investment strategies include:

Buy and Hold: Invest in assets with the intention of holding them for the long term, allowing them to appreciate over time. This strategy is often used for stocks and real estate.

Dollar Cost Averaging: Invest a fixed amount of money at regular intervals, regardless of market conditions. This strategy reduces the impact of market volatility.

Value Investing: Seek undervalued assets or companies with strong fundamentals, aiming to profit as their value appreciates.

Growth Investing: Invest in assets with the potential for above average growth, even if they have higher volatility.

Income Investing: Focus on investments that generate regular income, such as dividend paying stocks or bonds.

Asset Allocation: Diversify your investments across various asset classes, such as stocks, bonds, real estate, and cash, to manage risk and optimize returns.

4.3 Asset Classes

There are several asset classes in which you can invest. Each has its own riskreturn profile and is suited to different financial goals. Some common asset classes include:

Stocks: Ownership shares in publicly traded companies. Stocks have the potential for high returns but come with greater volatility.

Bonds: Debt securities issued by governments or corporations. Bonds offer regular interest payments and lower risk compared to stocks.

Real Estate: Investing in physical properties or real estate investment trusts (REITs) that own and manage real estate assets.

Mutual Funds and Exchange Traded Funds (ETFs): Investment vehicles that pool money from multiple investors to invest in a diversified portfolio of assets.

Commodities: Investing in physical goods like gold, oil, or agricultural products.

Alternative Investments: Includes hedge funds, private equity, and venture capital, which often require higher minimum investments and involve more complex strategies.

Cash and Cash Equivalents: Highly liquid assets like savings accounts and money market funds that provide capital preservation but typically offer lower returns.

4.4 Risk Management

Investing inherently carries risk, and understanding and managing risk is crucial to your success. Some risk management strategies include:

Diversification: Spreading your investments across different asset classes can help reduce risk by avoiding overexposure to a single investment.

Asset Allocation: Determine the right mix of assets based on your risk tolerance and financial goals.

Research and Due Diligence: Thoroughly research investments and assess their potential risks and returns.

Risk Tolerance: Assess your own risk tolerance, which is your ability and willingness to withstand investment losses without panicking.

Long Term Perspective: Take a long term view of your investments, which can help ride out market fluctuations and increase the likelihood of positive returns over time.

4.5 The Importance of a Long Term Perspective

Investing with a long term perspective is a key principle for achieving financial success. Short term market fluctuations are common, but history has shown that, over the long run, investments tend to appreciate. Benefits of a long term perspective include:

Compound Growth: Earning returns on your initial

investments, as well as on the returns themselves, can significantly boost wealth over time.

Reduced Emotional Reaction: A long term perspective can reduce the emotional stress associated with short term market volatility.

Time to Recover: In the event of market downturns, a long term horizon allows investments to potentially recover and grow.

4.6 Conclusion

Investing is a critical component of achieving early financial success and becoming a millionaire at a young age. It empowers your money to grow and work for you, providing opportunities for wealth accumulation and financial security. By developing a well-defined investment strategy, understanding different asset classes, managing risk, and maintaining a long term perspective, you can harness the power of investing to reach your financial goals.

In the upcoming chapters, we will continue to explore strategies and principles that complement your investment knowledge and contribute to your journey toward financial prosperity.

CHAPTER FIVE

5.0 Building Multiple Streams of Income

In this chapter, we will delve into the concept of building multiple streams of income—a powerful strategy for accelerating your journey towards financial success. Diversifying your income sources not only increases your earning potential but also provides greater financial stability and security.

5.1 The Significance of Multiple Streams of Income

Relying solely on a single source of income, such as a job, can limit your financial growth and leave you vulnerable to economic downturns. Building multiple streams of income is a proactive approach to financial security and wealth accumulation. Here's why it's crucial:

Increased Earning Potential: Multiple income streams

provide the opportunity to earn more money, allowing you to reach your financial goals faster.

Risk Mitigation: Diversifying your income sources reduces the risk associated with relying on one source. If one stream falters, others can provide a financial safety net.

Financial Security: Having multiple income streams can help you weather unexpected expenses, emergencies, or job loss with greater ease.

Wealth Accumulation: Income diversification accelerates wealth accumulation, enabling you to invest more and potentially achieve financial independence sooner.

5.2 Types of Income Streams

Building multiple streams of income involves generating revenue from various sources. Here are common types of income streams to consider:

5.2.1 Earned Income

Primary Job: Your primary source of income from a job or career.

Part Time Work: Taking on part time or freelance work in addition to your primary job.

5.2.2 Passive Income

Investments: Earnings from investments, such as dividends from stocks, interest from bonds, or rental income from real estate.

Royalties: Income generated from intellectual property, like books, music, or patents.

Online Businesses: Revenue from online ventures, such as ecommerce, affiliate marketing, or digital product sales.

5.2.3 Side Hustles and Businesses

Side Businesses: Operating small businesses or side hustles, such as consulting, coaching, or selling handmade products.

Entrepreneurship: Building and scaling your own business ventures.

5.2.4 Real Estate

Rental Properties: Earnings from owning and renting out residential or commercial properties.

Real Estate Investment Trusts (REITs): Dividends earned from investing in publicly traded REITs.

5.2.5 Investments

Stock Market: Capitalizing on equity investments and trading in the stock market.

Bonds: Generating interest income from fixed income securities.

Mutual Funds and ETFs: Earnings from professionally managed investment portfolios.

5.2.6 Intellectual Property

Books and Publications: Royalties from books, articles, and other written content.

Patents and Inventions: Licensing your inventions to earn royalties.

5.3 Building Multiple Streams of Income

Creating multiple income streams requires a strategic approach. Here's a step-by-step guide to help you get started:

5.3.1 Identify Opportunities

Evaluate your skills, interests, and passions to identify potential income generating opportunities.

Research different income streams and assess their feasibility and income potential.

5.3.2 Set Clear Goals

Define specific financial goals for each income stream. What do you want to achieve, and by when?

Prioritize your income streams based on your goals and the effort required.

5.3.3 Invest in Learning

Acquire the necessary knowledge and skills for each income stream. This might involve taking courses, gaining certifications, or seeking mentorship.

5.3.4 Start Small and Scale

Begin with a manageable side hustle or investment to gain experience and build confidence.

As you see success, reinvest earnings to scale your income streams.

5.3.5 Diversify

Aim for a balance of active and passive income sources to spread risk.

Diversify within each category (e.g., different types of investments, multiple income generating businesses).

5.3.6 Manage Your Time Wisely

Effectively manage your time to juggle multiple income streams without burning out.

Use productivity tools and time management techniques to stay organized.

5.4 Maintaining and Growing Income Streams

Building multiple income streams is an ongoing process. Here's how to maintain and grow them over time:

Regularly assess the performance of each income stream and make necessary adjustments.

Stay updated on industry trends and market conditions to identify growth opportunities.

Continue investing in your education and skill development to enhance your earning potential.

Reinvest profits from one income stream into others to accelerate growth.

5.5 Conclusion

Building multiple streams of income is a strategic approach to achieving financial success and becoming a millionaire at a young age. By diversifying your income sources and continuously growing them, you can increase your earnings, reduce financial risks, and secure a brighter financial future. In the following chapters, we will explore additional strategies and principles to complement your journey toward financial prosperity.

CHAPTER SIX

6.0 Networking and Mentorship

In this chapter, we'll explore the vital role that networking and mentorship play in your journey to financial success. Building strong professional relationships and seeking guidance from experienced mentors can provide valuable insights, opportunities, and support as you work toward becoming a millionaire at a young age.

6.1 The Power of Networking

Networking is the art of building and nurturing relationships within your industry or field of interest. Effective networking can open doors to various opportunities, including job offers, partnerships, investments, and valuable connections. Here's why networking is essential:

Access to Opportunities: Networking exposes you to job openings, investment prospects, and collaborations that you might not discover otherwise.

Knowledge Sharing: You can learn from others' experiences, insights, and expertise, accelerating your personal and professional growth.

Support System: A strong network provides emotional and professional support during challenging times, offering guidance and encouragement.

Resource Pooling: Networking allows you to tap into a pool of resources, from industry specific knowledge to potential investors.

6.2 Building a Network

Creating and maintaining a professional network takes time and effort. Here are steps to build and expand your network effectively:

6.2.1 Define Your Goals

Clarify your networking objectives. What do you hope to achieve through networking? Identifying your goals will help you focus your efforts.

6.2.2 Attend Events and Conferences

Attend industry related events, conferences, seminars, and workshops. These gatherings provide opportunities to meet likeminded individuals and industry leaders.

6.2.3 Join Professional Organizations

Become a member of relevant professional organizations, associations, or clubs. These groups often host networking events and provide access to industry resources.

6.2.4 Utilize Online Platforms

Leverage social media platforms like LinkedIn to connect with professionals in your field.

Participate in online forums, discussion groups, and communities related to your interests.

6.2.5 Networking Etiquette

Approach networking with a genuine interest in others.

Listen actively and engage in meaningful conversations.

Offer help and support to your connections when possible,

creating a reciprocal relationship.

6.2.6 Follow Up

After making initial connections, follow up with a personalized message or a thank you note. Maintain regular contact to nurture the relationship.

6.3 The Role of Mentorship

Mentorship involves a more experienced individual (mentor) providing guidance, support, and advice to someone seeking to grow in their career or achieve specific goals. Mentorship is invaluable for several reasons:

Learning from Experience: Mentors can share their experiences, helping you avoid common pitfalls and make informed decisions.

Expanding Your Network: A mentor's network can become accessible to you, providing valuable connections and opportunities.

Personal Growth: Mentorship can boost your

confidence, skills, and leadership abilities.

Accountability: Mentors hold you accountable for your goals and provide encouragement to stay on track.

6.4 Finding a Mentor

Finding the right mentor is essential for your growth and success. Here's how to identify and approach potential mentors:

6.4.1 Clarify Your Objectives

Define your specific goals and what you hope to gain from mentorship.

6.4.2 Identify Potential Mentors

Look for individuals who have achieved what you aspire to accomplish or possess expertise in areas where you seek guidance.

Explore your existing network and professional connections for potential mentors.

6.4.3 Reach Out Respectfully

Approach potential mentors with a clear and concise

request for mentorship, explaining why you value their guidance.

Be respectful of their time and availability, and express your willingness to reciprocate the favor.

6.4.4 Foster the Relationship

Establish a regular cadence for meetings or communication.

Be open to feedback and take action on the advice and insights provided by your mentor.

6.4.5 Give Back

Show gratitude to your mentor by sharing your progress and acknowledging their contributions to your growth.

6.5 Building a Supportive Network

Beyond finding a mentor, seek to build a supportive network of peers and colleagues who can offer advice, share experiences, and collaborate on projects. Surrounding yourself with positive and likeminded individuals can greatly contribute to your success.

6.6 Conclusion

Networking and mentorship are indispensable tools on your journey to financial success and becoming a millionaire at a young age. Cultivating a robust professional network can provide opportunities, knowledge, and support. Additionally, mentorship from experienced individuals can guide you, accelerate your growth, and offer valuable insights.

As you continue to expand your network and seek mentorship opportunities, remember that building and nurturing relationships should be authentic and mutually beneficial. In the following chapters, we will explore additional strategies and principles to complement your path towards financial prosperity.

CHAPTER SEVEN

7.0 Time Management

In this chapter, we delve into the critical skill of time management—an essential component of achieving early financial success. Effective time management empowers you to maximize productivity, make the most of your available hours, and maintain a balanced and sustainable approach to your journey toward becoming a millionaire at a young age.

7.1 The Value of Time

Time is your most precious resource. It's finite and irreplaceable. Understanding the value of time is fundamental to achieving your financial goals. Here's why time matters:

Opportunity Cost: Every moment spent on one activity

represents an opportunity foregone for another potentially more valuable activity.

Productivity Impact: Efficient use of your time can significantly boost your productivity, allowing you to accomplish more in less time.

Work Life Balance: Proper time management helps you maintain a healthy balance between work, personal life, and your financial pursuits.

7.2 Principles of Effective Time Management

Successful time management is grounded in principles that help you prioritize, plan, and execute your tasks efficiently. Here are key principles to consider:

7.2.1 Set Clear Goals

Define clear and specific financial goals that align with your aspirations.

Break down your goals into manageable tasks and prioritize them based on importance and urgency.

7.2.2 Prioritize Tasks

Distinguish between tasks that are urgent and those that

are important. Focus on tasks that align with your long term financial objectives.

Use techniques like the Eisenhower Matrix to categorize tasks by priority.

7.2.3 Time Blocking

Allocate specific blocks of time for different types of tasks or activities. For example, dedicate focused blocks for work, learning, networking, and relaxation.

Avoid multitasking, as it often reduces overall efficiency.

7.2.4 Learn to Say No

Be selective about taking on new commitments. Assess whether they align with your goals and whether you have the time and resources to fulfill them effectively.

Politely decline tasks or responsibilities that do not contribute to your financial objectives.

7.2.5 Delegate and Outsource

Delegate tasks that others can perform more efficiently or that do not require your expertise.

Consider outsourcing tasks like administrative work,

research, or even certain aspects of your business.

7.2.6 Use Technology Wisely

Utilize productivity tools, time tracking apps, and calendars to organize your schedule and set reminders. Leverage automation to streamline repetitive tasks.

7.2.7 Continuous Improvement

Regularly assess your time management strategies and seek ways to improve efficiency.

Reflect on your daily habits and adjust them to align with your goals.

7.3 Time Management for Financial Success

Effective time management is particularly crucial on your path to financial success. Here's how it can benefit your financial journey:

7.3.1 Efficient Learning

Allocate time for continuous learning and skill development, which can increase your earning potential. Set aside time for reading financial literature, attending webinars, and acquiring knowledge related to your financial goals.

7.3.2 Productive Work

Use time blocks for focused and productive work. Prioritize tasks that directly contribute to your financial objectives.

Minimize distractions and stay organized to maximize work efficiency.

7.3.3 Networking and Mentorship

Dedicate time to nurture your professional network and mentorship relationships.

Schedule regular meetings or interactions with mentors and peers to maintain and expand your network.

7.3.4 Financial Planning

Allocate time for financial planning, including budgeting, investment research, and goal tracking.

Regularly review your financial plan and adjust it as needed.

7.4 Maintaining Work Life Balance

While time management is crucial for financial success, it's equally important to maintain a healthy work life balance. Overworking can lead to burnout and hinder your long term productivity. Here are tips for achieving balance:

Schedule regular breaks to rest and recharge.

Dedicate time to family, friends, hobbies, and relaxation.

Set boundaries for work related tasks and avoid working excessively long hours.

7.5 Conclusion

Time management is a foundational skill for achieving early financial success and becoming a millionaire at a young age. By setting clear goals, prioritizing tasks, leveraging technology, and continuously improving your time management strategies, you can make the most of your time and optimize your efforts.

Remember that time is a finite resource, and how you use it can significantly impact your financial journey. In the upcoming chapters, we will continue to explore additional strategies and principles to complement your path toward financial prosperity.

CHAPTER EIGHT

8.0 Overcoming Challenges

In this chapter, we will discuss the inevitable challenges and obstacles you may encounter on your journey to becoming a millionaire at a young age. Overcoming these challenges requires resilience, adaptability, and a strategic approach. By understanding and addressing these obstacles, you can navigate the path to financial success more effectively.

8.1 Identifying Common Challenges

Before addressing challenges, it's essential to recognize the most common ones young individuals face on their quest for financial success:

8.1.1 Financial Constraints

Limited capital: Starting with minimal savings or resources can make it challenging to invest or launch a business.

8.1.2 Lack of Experience

Inexperience in managing finances or running a business

can lead to costly mistakes.

8.1.3 Risk Aversion

Fear of failure or taking risks can hinder entrepreneurial pursuits or investment decisions.

8.1.4 Work Life Balance

Balancing your financial ambitions with personal life, relationships, and self-care can be difficult.

8.1.5 Market Volatility

Economic downturns and market fluctuations can impact investments and business ventures.

8.1.6 Competition

Competition in the job market or business sector can be fierce, requiring unique strategies to stand out.

8.2 Strategies for Overcoming Challenges

Overcoming these challenges demands a combination of strategies, resilience, and adaptability. Here's how to address each of the common challenges:

8.2.1 Financial Constraints

Bootstrapping: Start small and gradually reinvest profits to grow your wealth or business.

Budgeting: Create a detailed budget to maximize your existing resources and prioritize savings.

Seek Funding: Explore options like loans, grants, or investment from family and friends.

8.2.2 Lack of Experience

Education: Invest in learning and gaining expertise through courses, books, and mentorship.

Start Small: Begin with manageable projects or investments to gain experience and confidence.

Mentorship: Seek guidance from experienced mentors who can provide insights and advice.

8.2.3 Risk Aversion

Risk Assessment: Analyze risks carefully and develop risk mitigation strategies.

Start Conservatively: Begin with less risky investments or ventures, gradually increasing your risk tolerance as you gain confidence and experience.

Mindset Shift: Embrace failure as a learning opportunity rather than a setback.

8.2.4 Work Life Balance

Prioritize Self Care: Allocate time for relaxation, exercise, and activities that rejuvenate you.

Time Management: Efficient time management can help you balance your personal life and financial pursuits.

Set Boundaries: Clearly define work hours and personal time to avoid burnout.

8.2.5 Market Volatility

Diversify Investments: Diversification can help spread risk across different assets.

Emergency Fund: Maintain an emergency fund to navigate financial setbacks.

Long Term Perspective: Understand that market fluctuations are normal, and a long term investment horizon can mitigate their impact.

8.2.6 Competition

Unique Value Proposition: Identify what sets you apart from the competition, whether in the job market or in business.

Continuous Learning: Stay updated with industry trends and emerging skills to maintain a competitive edge.

Networking: Leverage your professional network to discover opportunities and collaborations.

8.3 Resilience and Adaptability

Resilience and adaptability are invaluable qualities on your journey to financial success. They enable you to bounce back from setbacks, learn from failures, and adjust your strategies as needed. Cultivate these traits to navigate challenges effectively.

8.4 Seeking Support and Mentorship

Don't hesitate to seek support from mentors, advisors, or support groups. They can provide guidance, share experiences, and offer encouragement when faced with challenges. Mentorship, in particular, can be a powerful resource for overcoming obstacles.

8.5 Conclusion

Challenges are an integral part of any ambitious financial journey. Rather than viewing them as roadblocks, consider them as opportunities for growth and learning. By identifying common challenges, implementing strategies to overcome them, cultivating resilience, and seeking support when needed, you can overcome obstacles and continue moving toward your goal of becoming a millionaire at a young age.

In the following chapters, we will explore additional strategies and principles to further enhance your path toward financial prosperity.

CHAPTER NINE

9.0 Giving Back

In this chapter, we explore the importance of giving back and the positive impact it can have on your journey to becoming a millionaire at a young age. While your financial success is a priority, contributing to your community and causes you care about not only enriches your life but also plays a significant role in your overall success.

9.1 The Power of Giving Back

Giving back, whether through philanthropy, volunteering, or supporting charitable causes, has several compelling benefits:

9.1.1 Fulfillment and Purpose

Contributing to others' wellbeing can bring a deep sense of fulfillment and purpose to your life.

Knowing that your success can positively impact others can be a powerful motivator.

9.1.2 Positive Impact

Your contributions can make a meaningful difference in the lives of individuals or communities in need.

Addressing social and environmental issues can lead to positive change on a broader scale.

9.1.3 Networking and Relationships

Engaging in charitable activities often connects you with likeminded individuals and organizations.

These connections can open doors to new opportunities, both personally and professionally.

9.1.4 Reputation and Branding

Giving back enhances your reputation as a socially responsible and compassionate individual.

It can positively influence how others perceive you and your business endeavors.

9.2 Ways to Give Back

There are numerous ways to give back, and your approach can align with your interests, values, and resources. Here are some common ways to make a difference:

9.2.1 Charitable Donations

Contribute to nonprofit organizations or charities that resonate with your values.

Consider creating a structured giving plan to allocate a portion of your income or profits to charitable causes.

9.2.2 Volunteering

Offer your time and skills to charitable organizations or community projects.

Volunteering can be a handson way to make a direct impact and build meaningful relationships.

9.2.3 Mentorship and Education

Share your knowledge, expertise, and experiences with others who can benefit from your guidance.

Mentorship programs and educational initiatives can

empower individuals to achieve their goals.

9.2.4 Social Entrepreneurship

Consider launching or supporting businesses that have a social or environmental mission alongside profit.

Social entrepreneurship blends financial success with positive societal impact.

9.2.5 Impact Investing

Invest in businesses or projects that prioritize both financial returns and social or environmental goals.

Impact investing can align with your financial and philanthropic objectives.

9.3 Integrating Giving Back into Your Journey

Integrating giving back into your journey toward financial success involves thoughtful planning and a commitment to making a positive impact. Here's how to incorporate it effectively:

9.3.1 Define Your Values

Reflect on your core values and the causes or issues that

resonate with you personally.

Identify the ways in which you can align your financial success with these values.

9.3.2 Set Goals

Establish specific giving goals, such as the percentage of your income or profits you want to allocate to charitable efforts.

Define the impact you want to achieve through your contributions.

9.3.3 Research and Choose Causes

Research nonprofit organizations and causes to determine which align most closely with your values and goals.

Verify the legitimacy and impact of the organizations you plan to support.

9.3.4 Create a Giving Plan

Develop a structured giving plan that outlines how you will allocate your time, resources, and expertise.

Consider both short term and long term initiatives that

reflect your commitment to giving back.

9.3.5 Measure and Celebrate Impact

Implement systems to measure the impact of your contributions.

Celebrate milestones and achievements in your philanthropic endeavors.

9.4 The Ripple Effect

Giving back doesn't just benefit the recipients; it also creates a positive ripple effect in your life. The act of contributing to the wellbeing of others can enhance your personal and professional growth, strengthen your relationships, and inspire those around you to do the same.

9.5 Conclusion

Giving back is a powerful and meaningful component of your journey to financial success. It enriches your life, positively impacts others, and contributes to the greater good of society. By aligning your financial success with your values and committing to making a difference, you can achieve not only wealth but also a sense of purpose and fulfillment.

In the following chapters, we will continue to explore additional strategies and principles to complement your path toward financial prosperity, including wealth preservation and legacy planning.

CHAPTER TEN

10.0 Financial Freedom

In this final chapter, we delve into the concept of financial freedom—a state where your financial resources and passive income streams provide you with the freedom to live life on your terms. Achieving financial freedom is the ultimate goal for many on the path to becoming a millionaire at a young age.

10.1 Understanding Financial Freedom

Financial freedom is the ability to:

Cover your living expenses and desired lifestyle without needing to rely on a traditional job or active income source.

Have the freedom to make choices based on your preferences rather than financial necessity.

Pursue your passions, interests, and goals, whether they involve work, travel, philanthropy, or leisure.

10.2 The Path to Financial Freedom

While achieving financial freedom may seem like a daunting task, it's a realistic goal with the right strategies and mindset. Here's how to work towards financial freedom:

10.2.1 Define Your Financial Independence Number

Calculate the amount of passive income you need to cover your living expenses and desired lifestyle. This becomes your Financial Independence Number.

Consider factors like housing, food, healthcare, travel, and any other expenses relevant to your ideal lifestyle.

10.2.2 Create Multiple Income Streams

Build and diversify multiple income streams, such as investments, rental income, business ventures, or royalties.

Ensure these income streams are designed to be as passive

as possible, requiring minimal ongoing effort.

10.2.3 Reduce Debt and Expenses

Pay off high interest debt and reduce unnecessary expenses to increase your savings and investment capacity.

Budget and track your expenses to identify areas where you can cut back.

10.2.4 Invest Wisely

Continue to invest in assets that generate passive income, such as dividend stocks, real estate, or bonds.

Reinvest your earnings to accelerate wealth accumulation.

10.2.5 Build an Emergency Fund

Maintain an emergency fund to cover unexpected expenses and financial setbacks, ensuring your passive income remains untouched.

10.2.6 Develop a Wealth Preservation Plan

Consider strategies to preserve your wealth, such as estate planning, asset protection, and tax optimization.

Consult with financial advisors and legal professionals to create a comprehensive plan.

10.2.7 Monitor and Adjust

Regularly review your financial plan and make adjustments based on changes in your goals, circumstances, and market conditions.

Stay disciplined in your financial decisions, avoiding impulsive or emotional choices.

10.3 Achieving Financial Freedom at a Young Age

Becoming financially free at a young age requires dedication, discipline, and a long term perspective. Here are some additional considerations:

10.3.1 Aggressive Savings and Investment

Aim to save and invest a significant portion of your income, especially in the early years.

Maximize contributions to retirement accounts, take advantage of employer benefits, and explore tax efficient investment strategies.

10.3.2 Entrepreneurship and Passive Income

Pursue entrepreneurial ventures that can generate passive income streams.

Create and scale businesses that align with your interests and expertise.

10.3.3 Continuous Learning

Invest in your education and skill development to increase your earning potential and financial literacy.

Stay informed about investment opportunities and market trends.

10.3.4 Risk Management

Diversify your investment portfolio to mitigate risk.

Have a contingency plan in case of unexpected financial challenges.

10.4 Celebrate Milestones

As you progress towards financial freedom, celebrate milestones along the way. These achievements can provide motivation and reinforce your commitment to your financial goals.

10.5 The Freedom to Choose

Financial freedom is about having the freedom to make choices that align with your passions, values, and goals. It's not solely about accumulating wealth but using it as a tool to create the life you desire.

10.6 Conclusion

Achieving financial freedom and becoming a millionaire at a young age is a remarkable accomplishment. It requires a clear vision, disciplined financial habits, and a commitment to long-term planning. By defining your goals, diversifying income streams, managing expenses, and continually investing in your financial education, you can create a path to financial freedom that allows you to live life on your own terms.

In closing, remember that your journey to financial freedom is unique to you. Embrace the challenges, stay focused on your goals, and enjoy the journey as you work towards the ultimate freedom—financial independence.

CHAPTER ELEVEN

11.0 Case Studies

In this chapter, we will examine real-life case studies of individuals who successfully became millionaires at a young age. These stories provide insights into the strategies, challenges, and decisions that contributed to their financial success. By studying these cases, you can gain valuable lessons and inspiration for your own financial journey.

11.1 Case Study 1: Mark Zuckerberg

Background: Mark Zuckerberg, the cofounder of Facebook (now Meta Platforms, Inc.), became one of the world's youngest billionaires. He launched Facebook from his dorm room at Harvard University at the age of 19.

Key Strategies:

Innovative Idea: Zuckerberg identified a gap in the social networking market and created a platform that connected people globally.

Entrepreneurial Drive: He pursued his vision with relentless determination, attracting investors and expanding the platform's user base.

Adaptability: Facebook evolved and diversified, adding features like advertising and acquiring Instagram and WhatsApp.

Lessons:

Innovative ideas and determination can lead to extraordinary success.

Adaptability and continuous innovation are essential for long term growth.

11.2 Case Study 2: Kylie Jenner

Background: Kylie Jenner, a member of the KardashianJenner family, built a cosmetics empire with her company, Kylie Cosmetics. She became a billionaire at the age of 21.

Key Strategies:

Leveraging Personal Brand: Jenner used her fame and social media presence to promote her cosmetics line.

Product Development: She developed a line of products that resonated with her target audience.

Director Consumer Model: Kylie Cosmetics utilized online sales and marketing, reducing overhead costs.

Lessons:

Leveraging personal brand and social media can be powerful for business success.

Understanding your target audience and delivering what they want is crucial.

11.3 Case Study 3: Elon Musk

Background: Elon Musk, the CEO of SpaceX and Tesla, Inc., is known for his entrepreneurial ventures and rapid wealth accumulation. He became a billionaire in his 30s.

Key Strategies:

Visionary Goals: Musk pursued ambitious goals in space exploration and electric vehicles.

Risk Taking: He invested a significant portion of his wealth into ventures that others considered risky.

Innovation and Disruption: Musk's companies disrupted

established industries, including aerospace and automotive.

Lessons:

Bold vision and a willingness to take calculated risks can lead to substantial rewards.

Innovating and disrupting traditional industries can create enormous value.

11.4 Case Study 4: Warren Buffett

Background: Warren Buffett, often referred to as the "Oracle of Omaha," is a legendary investor who became a millionaire in his 30s and later one of the world's wealthiest individuals.

Key Strategies:

Value Investing: Buffett adhered to a value investing philosophy, focusing on undervalued stocks and long term investments.

Compound Interest: He utilized the power of compound interest by reinvesting dividends and earnings.

Patient Approach: Buffett maintained a patient and

disciplined approach to investing, avoiding impulsive decisions.

Lessons:

Value investing and a long term perspective can lead to significant wealth accumulation.

Compound interest can exponentially grow your wealth over time.

11.5 Conclusion

These case studies illustrate that there is no onesizefitsall approach to becoming a millionaire at a young age. Success can be achieved through various paths, including entrepreneurship, innovation, investing, and leveraging personal brand.

What these individuals share is a strong vision, determination, and a commitment to their goals. Their stories demonstrate that with the right strategies, resilience in the face of challenges, and a willingness to learn and adapt, you can achieve remarkable financial success, regardless of your age. Use these case studies as sources of inspiration and guidance as you continue your journey toward financial prosperity.

CHAPTER TWELVE

12.0 Conclusion

Congratulations on completing this journey through the chapters of "Becoming a Millionaire at a Young Age." Throughout this book, we've explored a wide range of principles, strategies, and insights aimed at guiding you on your path to financial success. As you conclude this journey, it's important to reflect on the key takeaways and consider how you can apply them to your own life.

12.1 Key Takeaways

Let's recap some of the fundamental lessons and concepts discussed in this book:

1. Financial Goal Setting: Clearly define your financial goals and create a roadmap to achieve them.

2. Financial Literacy: Invest in your financial education to make informed decisions about money and investments.

3. Entrepreneurship: Explore entrepreneurial ventures and opportunities to create income streams.

4. Investing: Develop a diversified investment portfolio and adhere to a long term perspective.

5. Time Management: Mastering time management is

essential for productivity and balance in your financial pursuits.

6. Networking and Mentorship: Building relationships and seeking guidance from mentors can open doors to opportunities.

7. Overcoming Challenges: Challenges are part of the journey; resilience and adaptability are key.

8. Giving Back: Consider the positive impact of giving back to your community and the world.

9. Financial Freedom: Work towards financial freedom, where your passive income covers your desired lifestyle.

10. Case Studies: Real life examples provide inspiration and insights into different paths to financial success.

12.2 Your Unique Journey

Remember that your journey to financial success is unique. While these principles and case studies provide valuable guidance, your circumstances, interests, and goals are distinct. Tailor the strategies and lessons to align with your individual path.

12.3 Continuous Learning and Adaptation

Financial success is not a onetime achievement; it's an ongoing process. Embrace the idea of continuous learning, adaptation, and growth. Stay informed about financial markets, industry trends, and emerging opportunities. Be open to adjusting your strategies as your circumstances evolve.

12.4 Persistence and Resilience

Persistence in the face of challenges and setbacks is a hallmark of successful individuals. Approach obstacles as learning experiences, and let them strengthen your resolve to reach your goals.

12.5 Building a Legacy

Consider the impact you want to leave behind. Building a legacy involves not only financial wealth but also the positive influence you have on others, the causes you support, and the values you uphold.

12.6 Conclusion

Your journey to becoming a millionaire at a young age is a significant undertaking that requires dedication, discipline, and a clear vision. Along the way, you'll experience highs and lows, but with the right mindset and strategies, you can achieve your financial aspirations.

As you move forward, remember that financial success is a means to an end—it should enhance your life and provide you with the freedom to pursue your passions and make a positive impact on the world. Keep your goals in focus, stay resilient, and never stop learning. Your path to financial prosperity is yours to create, and the future is filled with opportunities waiting for you to seize.

Thank you for embarking on this journey with us. We wish you success, fulfillment, and prosperity in all your financial endeavors.

ABOUT THE AUTHOR

OKAH ABRAHAM

Okah Abraham is an expert when it comes to real life experience and wealth building, he has giving out a lot of experience through writing to help others like yourself to be successful at early stage and with the right steps.

What makes this book unique is that everything inside are from personal and real life experience.

www.ingramcontent.com/pod-product-compliance
Lightning Source LLC
Chambersburg PA
CBHW062345290526
45794CB00005B/2107